Acclaim for *How to Cal*

"The wisdom of the East in user-friendly English. A powerful guide to stress reduction."

—Larry Payne, Ph.D.
director, International Association of Yoga Therapists,
and coauthor of *Yoga for Dummies* and *Yoga Rx*

"One of the very best books on relaxation, stress management, and concentration available for real people."

—John W. James
author of *The Grief Recovery Handbook*

"This simple yet practical book shows you how to calm down, become clear, and then perform at your best. It's truly amazing!"

—Brian Tracy
author of *Focal Point*

"Fred is a wonderful teacher. You will greatly benefit from his ideas!"

—Roger von Oech
author of *A Whack on the Side of the Head*

HOW TO CALM DOWN

Three Deep Breaths to Peace of Mind

FRED L. MILLER

Foreword by MARK BRYAN,
author of *The Artist's Way at Work*

WARNER BOOKS

NEW YORK   BOSTON

Warner Books

Time Warner Book Group
1271 Avenue of the Americas, New York, NY 10020
Visit our Web site at www.twbookmark.com.

Printed in the United States of America
First Warner Books Printing: January 2003
10   9   8   7   6   5   4   3   2

Library of Congress Cataloging-in-Publication Data
Miller, Fred L.
    How to calm down : three deep breaths to peace of mind / Fred L. Miller.
        p.cm.
    Includes bibliographical references.
    ISBN: 0-446-67971-2
    1. Respiration. 2. Breathing exercises. 3. Relaxation. 4. Stress management.
    I. Title.
    RA782.M554 2003
    155'042—dc21

2002023497

Text design by Meryl Sussman Levavi/Digitext

This book is dedicated to everyone who checks their watch two minutes after checking their watch, who flies through two dozen TV channels during one commercial break, or whose mother always said to them, "Slow down! You're gobbling your food."

Acknowledgments

Thank you to those who have helped me from the beginning, as well as along the way: Mildred and Lyle Miller, Kim Mandernach, Sidney Galanty, John Cholakis, John W. James, Marshall Karp, Gary Kraftsow, Ellen Kleiner, and Sharon Trocki-Miller. Most recently, Amye Dyer, Jackie Joiner, Noah Lukeman, Molly Chehak, and Warner Books, thank you!

Contents

Foreword by Mark Bryan   xi

An Introduction Worth Reading   xv

Part One   STARTING OUT   1

Chapter 1   Shifting Gears   3

Chapter 2   The Here and Now   11

Chapter 3   Countdown to Peace and Quiet   22

Chapter 4   Head Movies   29

Part Two	FINDING A POINT OF FOCUS	37
Chapter 5	Your Mind Thinks It's You	39
Chapter 6	Touch, Scent, and Taste	43
Chapter 7	Sound and Sight	50
Chapter 8	Living Breath	58
Chapter 9	Welcoming Words	65
Chapter 10	Practice until You Want to Practice	70

Part Three	GOING DEEPER	79
Chapter 11	What Else Is Cooking?	81
Chapter 12	The "M" Word	85
Chapter 13	The Stuff of the Universe	92
Chapter 14	Your Place in It All	97
Chapter 15	Tune in to Your Life	100

Notes	109
About the Author	111

Foreword

I first met Fred Miller ten years ago when my longtime mentor and dear friend Julia Cameron introduced him to me as a friend of hers. We spoke briefly, and I remember being particularly impressed by two things: one, that he was a yoga teacher, which surprised me because he looked more like a banker than an Indian mystic; and two, that he possessed a refreshing candor, saying what needed to be said in the immediate moment instead of reciting or expecting rote answers. It was Fred's character that first led me to him as a friend, and then as a teacher.

The power of *How to Calm Down* lies in its simplicity, as well as in Fred's uncanny ability to bring us to a new place before we realize we have left the old one. Because of this, I keep it on my desk for those days when a nasty blowup is lurking just beneath my emotional horizon, when I am living in the past or the future instead of the eternal moment, or when I need to flip my gratitude switch from a glass half empty to one half full.

I also find it comforting that Fred's techniques are thousands of years old and part of every major spiritual tradition, not just a modern psychological quick fix. As a result, they can be used and reused and somehow always remain fresh. It is the practicality and universality of the techniques that first attracted me to this book, and the kindness underlying each message that keeps me coming back for more. Compassion, as they say, is the highest value—and indeed, this book will introduce you to your more compassionate self.

As a teacher myself, I am acutely aware of other teachers. In fact, it was while watching Fred teach that I discovered endearing aspects of his character. He has the humor and compassion to guide students past their fears, and the confidence and strength to "stand in the fire" of students' doubts without relying on dogma to get them through the rough spots—all this while gently inviting them to become more fully who they really are.

Fred's combination of strength, grace, and commitment to "walk his talk" are why I asked him to join my teaching team years ago. Now, whenever possible, he takes part in the regular curriculum of the *Artist's Way at Work* seminars that I teach around the world. *How to Calm Down* is much like Fred's teaching: it meets you where you are and guides you easily through the experience of change. Before you know you have been taught anything, you are responding to the world differently from when you started, even if you were "absolutely, totally nuts" when you began.

Now take a deep breath, and enjoy.

MARK BRYAN

An Introduction Worth Reading

Would you like to feel better in less than ten seconds? If so, try the following exercise, called "Three Deep Breaths." As you do, keep your eyes open, and don't stop reading.

Inhale.
Now exhale.
Feels good, doesn't it?

Inhale again—a little deeper this time.
Now slow down your exhale. Stretch it out.

One more time—a long, slow inhale.

Pay attention as your breath comes in.

Don't think about it; just watch your breath as it fills your lungs.

Now the exhale—feel it, watch it. Exhale completely.

If you're anything like me, you never read the introductions to books. Instead, you scan the table of contents looking for the chapter that tells you how it's done, the secrets, the answers, the keys to the kingdom. Why? Because you want answers now! No use wasting time with "I was in the darkest night of my being when suddenly I saw the light."

So there's your answer. You now know how to calm down and how to use three deep breaths to bring peace of mind. In fact, this breath exercise will work for you anywhere, at any time.

Try doing it ten times in the next twenty-four hours—at work, on the phone, in the so-called express lane at the supermarket, in traffic, in an elevator, at a restaurant when your three-minute egg hasn't arrived after ten minutes. And don't worry, no one will know what you're doing.

PART ONE

Starting Out

I

Shifting Gears

At any given moment during a typical day, does your blood pressure rise, your pulse rate hit 10 percent over normal, and your breathing seem to stop? Sound familiar? If so, read on.

Once upon a time, I worked all day at a hamburger stand and went to school at night. It wasn't a bad job, but after eight hours of dealing with customers and coworkers, I was in no mood to concentrate in class. I had one hour between the end of work and the beginning of school. I was agitated and needed to calm down, to shift gears. I just didn't know how.

One day I tried taking a nap, and ended up missing school completely. Then I found another solution: two bottles of beer. I bought the beer at a store, parked my Volkswagen Bug in the school parking lot, and sat there drinking, all the while letting my mind wander. Random thoughts and worries ran their course through my brain and then left me alone. Sometimes I did take three deep breaths, but mainly because my belly was full of beer. Other times I would close my eyes and watch pictures play out in my mind. Or I would focus intensely on the cold, wet bottle, or on tearing the label off, leaving not a shred behind.

The beer solution worked. I calmed down. Better yet, the problems of the day vanished so completely that I could go to school and really hear what the teacher was saying. Because I was able to concentrate, I started doing well in class.

After a month, however, I had put on ten pounds. My clothes no longer fit, and I felt terrible. I knew I had to cut out my two bottles of beer, but I didn't know how to calm down without them.

I then began asking other people how to relax. They told me to go to Las Vegas. Go fishing. Get a date. None of these ideas would have helped me during that hour between work and school.

Other people's solutions were good for them, but not necessarily for me—something I'd already learned cooking hamburgers, where I'd have to stand for so long that my feet would be throbbing. As a result, I was always on the lookout for comfortable shoes to slip my big, wide feet into first thing in the morning. Anytime I'd see someone in a nice-looking pair of shoes, I'd ask if they were comfortable. The response was usually yes. Then I'd go to the shoe store and try on a pair, but inevitably they would hurt my feet.

I realized that I could not rely on other people for advice on shoes—or on relaxation, for that matter. I started noticing what I did when I was trying to calm down. Having abandoned the two-beer plan, I would smoke a cigarette, which seemed to help, though initially I could not figure out why. Smoking, it turned out, was an abbreviated version of what I had been doing in the school parking lot. First, I stopped whatever I was doing at the time—that is, I took a break. Next, my attention shifted from the jumble of thoughts racing through my mind to the one simple action of lighting a cigarette and taking a deep breath. Ahhh, relaxation.

All I was looking for when I began my quest for relaxation was peace of mind. I was frazzled. I wasn't running my life; instead, it was running me. I was the proverbial hamster scooting along as fast as I could on the wheel of life and forever losing the race. I needed a break.

What I found was much more than that. When I began practicing relaxation, my life began to change. I stopped "needing" things and became more productive. Sometimes in my life I have been fearful of new people or situations. Now I have developed more faith and confidence in myself, so much so that my outlook on life turned from negative to positive. Although I remain convinced that fear is part of the human condition, by regularly practicing relaxation, I found a way not to be stopped by fear but rather to move through it. Best of all, in learning to quiet my mind I came upon a calmness deep inside me. Reaching into that calmness, I could hear the voice of my true self, which is in tune with all things in the world—maybe even in the universe. In other words, I discovered that relaxation brings about a sense of well-being and contentment.

Coming up with an enjoyable approach to relaxation was not easy, however, especially since I had never stuck long with anything I didn't like. As with the shoes, I had to sift through a lot of styles that didn't work before finding one that did. After reading dozens of books and attending twice as many seminars on relaxation and stress management, I borrowed some methods and invented others. Then I synthesized the most effective ones into a series of short exercises, which you will find in the pages of this book.

If your partner, child, best friend, or doctor has been harping at you to calm down and relax, or if you yourself have been feeling the need for more serenity, then you will undoubtedly find some of these exercises helpful. They may even inspire you to *want* to relax. Best of all, you can practice them almost anywhere, even while sitting back in your easy chair. You do have an easy chair, don't you?

Before getting to more exercises, let's look at activities you may already be doing because you like them—relaxing pastimes, such as walking, reading, knitting. Do you like to go fishing, or play golf, or watch sports on TV? If so, chances are that this hobby serves as a way to relax.

Many people find, for example, that they calm down while out in nature. To some, being in nature means backpacking in the wilderness, whereas to others it means sitting in a lawn chair in the backyard while drinking a beer and turning a nice steak into a piece of charcoal. Maybe for you, being in nature means weeding the vegetables or planting daffodil bulbs. The important point to remember is that whatever helps you relax will also help you feel content, so do more of it. Unless of course your relaxing activity is eating chocolate and your pants size has gone from a 32-inch waist to a 38 and the bulk of your disposable income each month goes to the Hershey family. Like my two beers, some activities are relaxing momentarily, but ultimately unhealthy. We are looking for healthy, relaxing activities.

A 1989 visit to Monument Valley, along the Arizona–Utah border, made me feel wonderful. Maybe it was the sense I had of being a part of something larger than myself; or the vast spaces and massive red sandstone formations I'd seen in old western movies; or the clean air, blue sky, and huge clouds moving by. The only problem was that eventually I had to return to the workaday world. So what have I done to recapture the serenity I felt there? Every night before going to bed, I pull the lever on the La-Z-Boy and relax by conjuring up the feeling I had in Monument Valley. Now, such an idea may sound like I'm a half-bubble off level, but it works for me. And whatever works for you is the important thing.

I suggest that you find out exactly what helps you relax through your own experience. In the chapters that follow, you will read about a number of ways to relax. Try them all. Some will work for you; some won't. Some you'll like; some you won't. Use the ones that make a difference for you, and forget the others. Before long, you're sure to find that you have made life easier on yourself, that you've begun dictating the circumstances of your life rather than letting them control you.

This is where many books on relaxation fall apart. They ask you to believe in someone else's way of doing things. ("Yes, these shoes are very comfortable on me, so I'm sure you will like them.") The first relaxation books I read were from the Far East. Lavishly illustrated, they showed people with shaved heads and saffron robes, and came wrapped with incense or tapes of Tibetan monks chanting with a bell choir. For a while I was afraid I'd never learn to relax, because incense made me sneeze and I wasn't accustomed to being ceremonial; nor could I sit in the recommended cross-legged lotus position for hours at a time. But then I came upon the words of T. K. V. Desikachar, an internationally known yoga teacher from India, and I knew there was hope for me. He said, "East Indian forms of relaxation often are not suitable for Westerners. The technique a person uses must be compatible with their own culture."

I had let my own culture make me berserk. As I've described, my blood pressure was up, my pulse was 10 percent over normal (normal for me, that is), and my breathing was so shallow as to be hardly noticeable. But Desikachar's words were good news to me, and helped me understand that I didn't have to become a Hindu or a Buddhist or a yogi to learn to relax, and neither do you.

The only question is, what are you willing to do? The next few pages will show you the simple, easy things I did to learn to calm down. If I can do it, so can you. Just try a couple of the exercises; most of them are actually fun. I know you'll find at least one you like and that you are willing to do regularly. Most important, enjoy!

2

The Here and Now

Let me first ask you a question:

Do you really want to relax?

Don't you work better when you have a full head of steam? Think that question through and you will realize that the answer is, not necessarily. Sometimes a full head of steam is too much and actually gets in your way. You can call this relaxation stuff preventive medicine, or if that's too namby-pamby, you can think of it as being race-tuned. Do you change the oil in your car every 3,000 miles or do you drive it full speed until the engine blows up? What do you think the guys at the Indy 500 do?

Stephen Covey, in his book *The 7 Habits of Highly Effective People,* lists the most important habit last. Habit 7 is "Sharpen the saw," which roughly translates to keeping ourselves in peak condition—not running on empty, but being race-tuned. To do this we can implement two of Mr. Covey's other habits: Habit 3, "Put first things first," which in this case means taking care of ourselves first so we are in top shape, and Habit 1, "Be proactive"—not waiting for illness or a breakdown from overwork, but rather setting up a simple program that keeps us mentally race-tuned.

How can you achieve this? By focusing on the moment. The task itself does not matter—you could be frosting a cake or hanging a picture—as long as you're focused on it. But let your mind wander and you just might end up frosting the cat or smashing your thumb.

If you were walking in the woods, you probably wouldn't need to learn to relax, since you'd already be paying attention from one moment to the next. But suppose you're on a fishing or camping trip, and your mind goes off on a trek of its own. Anytime your thoughts wander over to the lake where you spent the previous day, or to the site where you hope to pitch your tent the following evening, call them back to the place you are in. When your mind drifts off and begins reliving yesterday or planning for tomorrow, bring it back to the present moment. Do everything you can to stay in the here and now.

If you can get to the woods, why you went there in the first place does not matter. Anyone can relax in the woods—a hunter looking to bag this season's buck or a vegetarian photojournalist. The woods don't care; the trees don't discriminate. Just being in the forest is what's relaxing. As the late-nineteenth-century naturalist John Muir said, "The clearest way into the Universe is through a forest wilderness."

Suppose you've been standing at the bus stop since 5:55 A.M. waiting for the 6:02. You look at your watch, again, and it's 6:15. That means you've been standing there for twenty minutes and still no bus. Does your mind jump back to yesterday, when you were late because you overslept, or forward to your potentially tardy arrival this morning? Probably, but what good does it do you? The bus still hasn't arrived.

Interestingly, the human mind is capable of over 60,000 thoughts a day, and, given free rein, more than 90 percent of them are the same ones you had the day before. Repeatedly reliving the past can keep you stuck in old worries, fears, and frustrations. Paying attention to what's around you, on the other hand, will snap you back to what's happening right now.

When casting off in a small sailboat, it's best to ride out with no outside thoughts, concentrating only on the wind, the water, and the course you have set. When you're sailing, you're sailing. When you're fretting about the leaky roof at home, you're not going to know when to come about...and you're certainly not relaxing.

Do you like to cook? Isn't it all-absorbing to give your full attention to chopping and mixing one ingredient at a time?

Gardening is another engaging task. Have you ever gone out to work in the garden for "just five minutes" and later looked at your watch to find that an hour had passed? Free of worries and cares, you had been thinking only of the soil and the plants. Very calming, isn't it? Try watering your garden not to get it over with, but simply to water—and to enjoy the experience of it.

Computers can be just as captivating. Have you ever had

ten minutes to kill and decided to check your e-mail? If you're anything like me, you'll wander onto the Internet and the next thing you'll hear is your wife saying, "We were supposed to leave half an hour ago. What are you doing in there?"

Can you go to a baseball game and think of nothing but baseball from the first pitch to the seventh-inning stretch? That too is a form of paying attention one moment at a time. Yogi Berra, who understood this principle from the other side of the dugout, once asked, "How can you think and hit at the same time?"

Or perhaps you are a musician. If so, have you ever played your favorite piece of music and thought of nothing else from start to finish? Guess what? You're relaxing! In such instances, relaxation has enormous rewards. Pianist Artur Schnabel once remarked, "The notes I handle no better than many pianists. But the pauses between the notes—ah, that is where the art resides."

Similarly, can you listen to your favorite piece of music and think of nothing else from the first note to the last? Listening one note at a time is enormously relaxing and a good way to practice paying attention. How about solo rock climbing? It's not a good idea to be thinking about tomorrow's lunch when you are scaling a 300-foot vertical rock face. If you want to live to eat tomorrow's lunch, you had better keep your mind on what you're doing! The same degree of concentration, with a cool head and clear thinking, is needed if you are closing a tough sale or trying to talk your boss into doing something your way.

*

Stress and tension clog up our minds with useless thoughts. Who has stress and tension? Nearly everyone. Why? Because most of us don't know how to release the steam that accumulates inside us day after day.

Have you ever caught yourself thinking that you are the only safe driver on the highway—that all the others are crazy and are trying to kill you by cutting you off and then slamming on their brakes? A near-accident can make you tense, sending a jolt through your nervous system. When you are scared of becoming another roadside fatality, even if the fear lasts only a second, your body senses danger and instantly floods your bloodstream with adrenaline. Your heart starts to race, your blood pressure skyrockets, and you prepare for action.

This fight-or-flight response once served a useful purpose. A prehistoric caveman, upon suddenly meeting up with a saber-toothed tiger, needed lots of adrenaline to make his next move. Heart thumping, veins bulging, he would either tangle with the creature or run for his life, and in the process release the "steam" that got him going.

People in danger today, however, can neither fight nor flee. When we're stuck in traffic, we cannot get out of the car and slug the driver who cut us off, and we certainly can't run away. Actually, there is no physical outlet for our extra adrenaline, no release valve for our rapidly pumping hearts.

Here's another example of how we get caught in our own steam. Joe's boss is giving him a hard time. Maybe Joe made a mistake—or worse yet, the boss made the mistake and blamed it on him. In any case, Joe is showing definite signs of a fight-or-flight response. But if he punches out his boss or if he heads for the door muttering, "Take this job and shove it!" chances are he'll be fired. Like many of us, Joe can't find a way to stabilize his nervous system without sacrificing his livelihood. And joblessness is unlikely to decrease anyone's stress levels.

The least destructive way out of this mess is through relaxation. Not only does relaxation help release the steam that builds up inside us every time we're trapped in a fight-or-flight predicament, it can also relieve the headaches, neck cramps, and shoulder pains sustained in our daily pursuit of survival. Relaxation lowers the blood pressure and almost immediately slows the heart rate, decreasing the chances of a heart attack. Over time, lower blood pressure and a slower heart rate add up to more good news: decelerated aging. That means you won't feel like a sixty-year-old when you're only thirty-five.

If the notions of blood pressure and heart rate are too abstract to understand in the midst of a chaotic day, look at it this way: calming down leads to a better night's sleep. Relaxing before sleep can help you wake up feeling rested. Not unwinding before sleep will leave you tired and stressed out, increasing the wear and tear on your body. And where are you going to live when your body wears out? From this perspective, high stress is tantamount to slow suicide, whereas less stress plus better sleep equals a longer life.

Here's the short-range view: relaxation can increase your energy, boost your health, and improve your memory, learning ability, and relationships with other people. Why? Because a calm mind leads to a healthy body, clear thinking, and better social interactions. With less mind fatigue, I find I have more energy to devote to myself and my loved ones. The more attention I give to myself and others, the better I feel. It's also true that when my mind is not clogged up with useless thoughts, I am more easily able to remember important information and to open myself to new experiences and learning. In this sense, relaxation improves the quality of life.

At this point, you may be wondering, "So if I want a longer, healthier, and happier life, all I have to do is take a walk in the park every day?"

The answer is: yes!

✳

To get a sense of the useless thoughts that fill your head with steam, try "Not Thinking" (Exercise I). The results are sure to be memorable.

Exercise I
NOT THINKING

This exercise will show you how thinking can distract you from relaxing. Read it through first, then give it a try.

- Sit comfortably, whatever that means for you. Kick back on the couch, with your feet on a hassock, or pull the lever on your recliner.
- Take three deep breaths, as described in the introduction. (Inhale, then exhale. Inhale more deeply, stretching out the exhale. Inhale even more deeply, paying attention to your breath, then exhale completely, feeling the breath leave your lungs.)
- Breathing slowly and easily, close your eyes, and for one full minute, don't think.

How did it go... not so hot? Was your mind racing for fifty-nine and a half of the sixty seconds? If so, congratulations—you're a human being! We all have minds that want to race a mile a minute, hurtling out of the here and now and into the there and then. Thinking is the enemy of relaxation.

When I first started practicing this exercise, my mind was full of chatter—my voice, my wife's, my boss's, the last song I'd heard on the radio. I was having conversations, even arguments, with people who weren't in the room with me! Not wanting to hear those voices yakking at me anymore, I decided to find something to do to quiet my mind. The simple techniques described in the next several chapters did the trick.

It will get better, the yakking will slow down...that's a promise.

3

Countdown to Peace and Quiet

When my mom's life wasn't going her way, she would say, "That person [situation] makes me nervous." Then her voice would inch up a little higher, her words would tumble out a bit faster, and a hint of hysteria would creep in. While watching her get annoyed on the outside and miserable on the inside, I would think, "Mom, calm down." But saying those words to her would have been like telling my dog Cookie not to dig in the backyard…useless. Agitation was ingrained in Mom's nature.

Oddly enough, my mother often told me to have patience. "I don't have it," she would admit. "I've never been a patient person—but you should be."

"How can I do that?" I'd ask.

"Count to ten," she'd always say.

Because she never counted to ten, I was always baffled by the "Do as I say, not as I do" message. Usually, I forgot to count, and as a result I was miserable. But sometimes I did count to ten, and occasionally it worked.

As an adult searching for ways to quiet the mind chatter going on inside me, I discovered that all the mind needed was something to keep it busy. Then I arrived at an exercise that worked more often than it didn't—and sure enough, it was a mind-absorbing variation on counting to ten.

Exercise II
QUIETING THE MIND BY COUNTING BACKWARD

Here you are going to count backward from fifteen to zero with your eyes closed. Read through the instructions first so you'll know what to do. This exercise will take less than one minute.

- Sit comfortably and close your eyes. Then take three deep breaths to calm down and clear your mind.
- Breathing easily, inhale. Now exhale, silently saying, "Fifteen."
- Inhale again. This time while exhaling, silently say, "Fourteen."
- Continue inhaling and counting down a number with each exhale.
- After you reach zero, take a few gentle breaths, all the while noticing how you feel. When you are ready, open your eyes.

Try Exercise II. Were the results better than those of Exercise I? Were there fewer random thoughts clogging up your mind? Most people find it easier to count down than to try to stop thinking. Why? Because the mind is more "reined in" when it has a task to perform.

Counting is a simple task, and certainly a lot safer than solo rock climbing. As such, it is a risk-free way to practice concentrating. Yes, while counting backward, the mind can drift off to other thoughts, as you may have found, but it will come quickly back to the business at hand. Better yet, while concentrating on this task, you cannot also be thinking about people or situations that make you nervous. As a result, you will be more relaxed. Vary this exercise by changing the numbers, counting down from eighteen to three, for example, or from thirty-three to sixteen. This will help keep your mind occupied.

Relaxation happens between thoughts. But with 60,000 thoughts a day, most of which consist of mind chatter, we don't have much time left over for relaxation. To pave the way for more "downtime," we must clear the mind of the chatter.

As you may have already experienced, clearing the mind is not as easy as it sounds. For example, while counting backward, did you start to fall asleep? Many people do. It's like sitting down to write a letter that you know is going to be difficult, and becoming drowsy as soon as you set pen to paper. Your next thought is, "Let me take a nap. Then I'll be able to write this letter." The problem in both instances is that the mind would rather go to sleep than engage in a difficult task. When faced with a simple task, however, the mind does not want to let go of thinking, even for a moment. The solution? Concentrate sharply on the counting and you won't fall asleep.

Here's another mind trick: by the end of the exercise, were you counting backward and thinking at the same time? This maneuver is similar to what happens after we learn to drive a car. At first, it takes all our concentration to work the gearshift and drive a short distance; but a year later, we can burn up the highway and hardly think about the fact that we're driving a vehicle. By then, the mind has the shifting of gears down so completely that it wants to do something else... such as think! It wants to rewrite the outcomes of yesterday's scenarios or strategize for tomorrow's.

When I started practicing relaxation, I preferred an agitated state of mind to a calm one. Being nervous was comforting, because it's what I was used to. I wanted to stay pissed off at people who had crossed my path. Only with a little more experience in relaxation did I discover how much it paid off, provided that I had the willingness to practice and the courage to change old habits.

What I found was that clearing the mind is like exercising a muscle: the more you work it, the stronger it gets. With practice, your mind will drift off less frequently, stay away for shorter periods of time, and come back more easily. For now, simply notice when your mind has strayed off and ask it to come back to counting.

Years ago, Harvard University Medical School published a report stating that counting backward lowers a person's blood pressure and heart rate. This means that if you're agitated and begin breathing deeply, counting down from fifteen with each exhale, you will instantly let off steam and calm down. If you don't have time for the countdown, at least stop and take the three deep breaths.

Practice both of these relaxation techniques day and night, preferably when you're not angry. That way, anytime you start to get upset you'll soon be able to achieve the state of mind my mom could only talk about. The three deep breaths will calm you down in less than ten seconds. Counting backward from fifteen to zero will relieve even more layers of stress in less than sixty seconds.

POINTS TO REMEMBER

Your mind loves to think.

If you give your mind a task to carry out, it will quiet down—at least for a while.

Once your mind has learned the task, it will give it back to you to do and will go on thinking.

To strengthen your mind's ability to clear itself of chatter, practice breathing and counting backward.

4

Head Movies

Did you ever want to make a movie? This chapter describes several "head movies" to try on for size. Movies in your head—sometimes called visualizations—provide a sure-fire way to chill out in a heated moment; to ease into sleep, or back to sleep, after a ghastly day; or to defuse an upsetting situation.

Remember how I relax by imagining myself in Monument Valley? Well, you can immerse yourself in the same sort of experience by taking a trip to the beach. Join me on this two-minute excursion, then create a "vacation getaway" of your own.

Exercise III
A TRIP TO THE BEACH

Read through this exercise once, then go back and "talk yourself" through it.

- Pull the lever on your recliner, close your eyes, and take three deep breaths.
- Imagine yourself sitting at the seashore. See the blue sky, the green water, the clouds overhead.
- Watch the waves as they roll in, break, and recede. Get into the easy, gentle rhythm of the waves.
- See the white sand around you. Feel it.
- Now feel the warm sun on your back and shoulders.
- Feel a cool breeze on your face.
- Smell the sea air.
- Smile. Let this pleasant scene relax you.

- Taste the salt in the air.
- Listen to the waves as they crash against the shore and roll back out again. Hear a seagull cry in the distance.

The more senses you call into action, the more this beach scene will calm you down. Why? Because your mind will be fully absorbed in the head movie—focused on seeing, feeling, smelling, tasting, and hearing the imaginary world around you.

Next time you need to chill out, close your eyes, take three deep breaths, and imagine yourself at the beach; using all your sense memories, see, feel, smell, taste, and hear the seashore. Or take your mind to a forest, or a mountain meadow. It makes no difference whether you go to a place you've been to before or one you've dreamed about. What matters is that you remember to use all your sense memories.

✳

Head movies can be a special treat before bedtime. Exercises IV and V will help you drift peacefully off to sleep.

Exercise IV
TOES TO NOSE

To unwind before going to sleep, turn off the TV, pull the lever on your recliner, and begin this exercise. It can also be performed while lying in bed with your eyes closed.

- Kick off your shoes, take three deep breaths, and relax your feet, from your toes all the way back to your heels.
- Slowly working your way upward, relax your calves, thighs, buttocks, and abdomen.
- Relax your lower back, chest, upper back, shoulders, and neck.
- Relax your face, releasing all tension from your chin, jaw, ears, and nose. Calm the inside of your head too, quieting the mind chatter.

While performing this exercise, you may discover that your feet are sore or your lower back aches. Sometimes simply becoming aware of such aches and pains will help your body relax. Other times you can heal discomfort by "breathing into" the area while focusing on it.

Exercise V
A WALK IN THE WOODS

This visualization is best performed with your eyes closed, so read through it once before trying it. Use it not only to help you fall asleep but also to assist you in getting back to sleep when you have awakened during the night.

- Close your eyes, take three deep breaths, and imagine yourself walking along a path in the woods. See the brown bark of the trees, smell their green leaves. Feel the warm sun on your back. Hear the birds chirping.
- Walking deeper into the woods, see the blue sky and white clouds. Feel a cool breeze on your cheeks and the softness of the ground under your feet.
- Walking deeper and deeper into the woods, hear a twig snap underfoot.
- As you round a bend, notice a cabin nestled among the trees. See wisps of smoke floating out of the chimney. Smell the fragrant wood burning in the fireplace. This is your cabin.
- Approach the cabin, open the door, and step inside. The

fireplace on the far wall is crackling with golden-orange flames. In front of it is a thick rug, and folded up at one end of this rug is your favorite blanket.

- Close the door behind you and walk over to the fireplace. Warm your body, front and back. Stretch out on the rug, feeling very comfortable, safe, and contented. Covering yourself with the blanket, drift off to a peaceful sleep.

Head movies have a way not only of lifting us off to paradise or dreamland but also of taking the sting out of our thoughts about uncomfortable real-life situations. As you practice Exercise VI, notice the change in your stress levels.

Exercise VI
AS YOU THINK, SO YOU FEEL

Here you can see the power of your thoughts in action. Read this exercise slowly before trying it.

- Sit back, close your eyes, take three deep breaths, and think about something that makes you happy, such as a hobby, your partner, or your pet. If you know how to take your pulse at your wrist or the side of your neck, do so. If not, simply notice how good you are feeling.

- See, in your mind's eye, a place you dread going to—such as your office or the dentist's, a classroom, or perhaps a courtroom.
- Slowly approach the building. As you do, feel your discomfort increasing. Your heart rate may be picking up, or tension may be creeping into your neck and shoulders.
- Keep watching as you open the door. See your boss, or whoever the biggest "pain in the neck" may be in this scene. Can you feel your neck muscles tightening, or your hands trembling ever so slightly? Take your pulse once again—is it faster this time?
- Before doing anything else, take three deep breaths.
- Go back to thinking about what makes you happy, or take another trip to the beach.

At this point, you should be feeling better. Moreover, you now have proof that you can take action to change your thinking, and that changing your thinking will alter how you feel. Think fearful thoughts and your stress level will rise; use head movies to concentrate on pleasant thoughts and it will drop.

Too much stress, as we know, is lethal. The hour of greatest concern is 9 A.M. Monday mornings, when more stress-related deaths occur than at any other time of the week. This means that if you regularly begin your week in a setting that puts a crick in your neck, you would be wise to tune in to a head movie. Relax first thing on Monday morning and you'll lessen your chances of imminent illness, injury, or death.

But don't wait until Monday morning. Many people get the Sunday night blahs just thinking about the next day. If you do too, create a movie in your head to reframe the situation at work. See things going pleasantly for you the next day. See yourself getting along well with the boss, your coworkers, and clients. See how well you can get along with the person who's been a pain in the neck. In short, create a head movie that helps you have a better working situation.

With practice, these exercises will become easier to use. Then the more you use them, the more they will enhance your life.

If what you want is a longer, happier, healthier life, you can stop reading here. If you want more, an even deeper experience of life than most people achieve, read on...

PART TWO

Finding a Point of Focus

5

Your Mind Thinks
It's You

Now that you know how to calm down, we're going to explore a few easy techniques for holding a point of focus. It was when I started to practice holding a point of focus that I felt a deeper calm and more self-confidence. As you work with these exercises—or at least the ones you like most—you will not only quiet your mind in the moment but also begin to experience an inner peace and an easier life. These are the lasting effects of relaxation.

Let's start by looking at the mind. My mind, scattered and

full of thoughts, resembles a wild horse. Attempting to concentrate on something is like trying to tame that horse; if you approach it with anything as confining as a saddle, it is apt to run away. You see, my mind is tricky. It flees from constraints. It learns new tasks, teaches them to me, then goes about its business of thinking other thoughts. In short, it does what it wants to do.

Your mind probably does too. Your seat of intelligence and reason fancies itself not only in charge of your thinking, but the beginning and end of everything you say and do. In other words, your mind thinks it's you.

Contrary to your mind's highfalutin notions, however, there is more to you than this ticker tape of thinking. If you occupy your mind with a task and slip past it, other parts of you will rise to the surface, such as your instinct and intuition. Instinct is what athletes rely on when they let the body take over. A good golfer will swing the club and send his tee shot straight down the fairway without thinking through the maneuver. He's confident that his body instinctively knows how to hit the ball. With the mind out of the way, golf can be enormously relaxing, but with the mind choreographing the strokes, golf can be stressful enough to cause a heart attack. The outcome depends on how you approach the game—and on how you approach your life.

Intuition bubbles up like a little voice in your ear when you start listening to your heart or your gut. Think of it as a sixth sense that overrides logical solutions that, somehow, you know won't solve the problem at hand. The more you quiet your mind, the more clearly and the more often will you hear the voice of intuition.

To get your mind out of the way enough to follow your instinct or hear the voice of intuition, you don't need to harness it; just give it a single point of focus. Each of the exercises in the next four chapters will teach you to hold one point of focus—such as one picture in your mind's eye, one sound in your mind's ear—and to stay with it. Anytime your mind drifts away from this single point you've chosen and you begin to notice a thought unfolding into an entire TV miniseries, you will have this point to come back to, something to refocus on. With practice, you will be able to achieve what you want at will...quite literally, a little peace of mind.

Here are two final thoughts to consider before getting rid of your mind. First, approach each exercise as an experiment. T. K. V. Desikachar, quoting his father, T. Krishnamacharya, the father of modern yoga, told me that as a teacher, his job is to find the one technique that suits each individual student. The teachings are for the students, not the teacher. He wrote in his book *The Heart of Yoga,* "Start with something to which you can relate. You must begin where you are—that's why I suggest you choose a technique that suits your temperament."[1] The fact is that you may not like all these techniques, or even half of them. If you like one, however, then that's the one for you.

Second, no matter how out of control your everyday world may be, don't expect it to vanish. The practice is not an escape or a retreat, but rather will lead you into the light of reality. We see the results of practice in our daily life, in our relationships and our tolerance of others.

Similarly, the purpose of practicing these point-of-focus exercises is not to hide from life. On the contrary, practicing them will bring you more into your life so that you can live it fully.

6

Touch, Scent, and Taste

Feeling, smelling, and tasting are strong, immediate senses. We'll begin holding one point of focus by working with each of them in turn.

ONE POINT OF TOUCHING

During one of the many times I tried to quit smoking, someone gave me a small, flat stone. "Treat it like Greek worry beads," he advised me. "When you want a cigarette, rub the stone." In the short run, it worked. Many times when I was thinking about having a cigarette, I would take the stone out of my pocket and hold it, look at it, then turn it over and over in my hand. After I'd spent a few seconds holding the stone, the urge for a cigarette would pass. Why? Because I couldn't think about the stone and a cigarette at the same time.

In the long run, I started smoking again, since there's more to staying off cigarettes than merely taking your mind off them for a few seconds at a time. In the longer run, however, I quit for good. Even so, I still carry a small stone with me. Every time I reach into my pocket for change, the stone is there to remind me that I can clear my mind by holding it. If I'm feeling nervous or annoyed, into my pocket I go to stop the rumbling in my head.

Connecting tactilely to an object may be the easiest point of concentration we have. Because the sense of touch is so engaging and convincing, it has been incorporated into a variety of devotional rituals. People of many different religions, for example, hold strings of beads and, while fingering each one, recite a designated prayer to go with it.

To experiment with touch as a point of focus, try Exercise VII. First you'll need to select an object from your surroundings, such as a lucky charm, a talisman, or a stone.

Exercise VII
TOUCHING AN OBJECT

- Sit quietly, holding your chosen object, and take three deep breaths.
- Closing your eyes, concentrate on the object in your hand.
- Whenever you notice your thoughts starting to drift off, squeeze or rub the object to bring your attention back to it.
- When you are ready, take a few deep breaths and open your eyes.

If your object is small, try carrying it around with you and practicing this exercise spontaneously. A larger object can be left at home in plain sight to serve as a reminder to keep practicing.

ONE POINT OF SMELLING

For many people scent ushers in the strongest sensory impressions. Until recently, I was not one of these people. In fact, I couldn't remember a smell at all until a teacher asked me to describe my grandmother's kitchen. Right away, I recalled the aroma of fresh cornbread. Next, I could see it cooling in a covered cast-iron skillet on the stove.

What did your grandmother's kitchen smell like?—baked casseroles, fresh pies, spices? Or how about a favorite aunt's kitchen, or a best friend's? If you've never spent much time in kitchens, try to recall the perfume or cologne worn by your last date or a special person in your life. Somewhere there is a fragrance you once loved, and right now you can smell it. Scent evokes powerful memories.

To work with smell as a point of focus, try Exercise VIII. It will help you concentrate on smells in your immediate environment that may soon become calming memories in your mind. Before beginning this exercise, scan the room for a delectable aroma, or set a bouquet of flowers nearby to serve as your point of focus. If you need something stronger, light a scented candle or burn a stick of incense.

Exercise VIII
TUNING IN TO SMELL

- Sit quietly and comfortably and take three deep breaths.
- Closing your eyes, concentrate on your chosen aroma.
- Briefly let your mind run wild with thoughts. Between thoughts, let your mind come back to the aroma.
- Now begin to focus only on the aroma. Anytime you notice yourself drifting into thinking, direct your concentration back to the scent, your one point of focus.
- When you are ready, take some deep breaths and open your eyes.

After just a few minutes of concentrating on a smell, you are likely to find that your thoughts have slowed down and your mind is a little quieter. If so, your sense of smell may be highly developed—in which case you'll want to keep aroma in mind whenever you feel the need to calm down.

ONE POINT OF TASTING

Have you ever seen a plate of food arranged so attractively you could almost taste it? Have you ever smelled an aroma so strongly you thought you could taste it, such as garlic roasting in olive oil or salt in the sea air at low tide?

Taste, a captivating sense, is able to gain our attention through sight and smell even before our taste buds are engaged. Once they do connect with a morsel of any sort, the sensation of taste is relatively short-lived, unless it's sustained through touch and smell. For example, how often have you felt the first soothing rush of flavor from a breath mint, only to forget about it seconds later? Many of us disregard that mint in our mouth until we've crunched the last speck of hardness between our back teeth.

What happened between the first burst of flavor and that last crunch? We lost conscious contact with the mint because we stopped concentrating on it! Had we touched it with our tongue and smelled its aroma wafting up from our mouth, we could have prolonged the taste experience and the calmness it awakened.

The next exercise will help you give the sense of taste your full attention. This time the prop you will need is a LifeSaver—either red, green, yellow, orange, or white, whichever is your favorite.

Exercise IX
TASTE: A VERITABLE LIFESAVER

- Sit comfortably and take three deep breaths. Then pop the LifeSaver into your mouth.
- As best you can, focus on the taste of the candy—the cherry, lime, lemon, orange, or pineapple flavor.
- While concentrating on the taste, resist the temptation to chew. (Sucking the candy can result in a longer period of focused attention, so see if you can keep it going this way.)
- When the LifeSaver has fully dissolved, notice how much fun you've had calming down.

7

Sound and Sight

If you are accustomed to using your ears and eyes, then these organs of perception are already fine-tuned enough to focus on one point. Your ears are well-trained in concentrating on sound. Similarly, your eyes have been sending messages to your mind for years. It's just a small jump to go from hearing or seeing to a deepened state of relaxation.

ONE POINT OF HEARING

One summer I lived in a beach house nearly at the water's edge. Each night, I could hear the surf breaking lightly on the sand. The more I listened to it, the more I relaxed. Come fall, I returned to city life, where the sound of the waves was replaced by the noise of car horns and jackhammers.

If you're lucky enough to be living in a beach house year round, or to have a babbling brook in your backyard, or to be within walking distance of a perpetual waterfall, you can close your eyes and endlessly take in the soothing sound of moving water. But in the event that your only source of continuously running water is your toilet, you'd be better off going to the music store and buying a tape of environmental sounds. If a summer rainstorm brings back memories of the best days of your childhood, then that's the tape for you. Soothing music is another possibility, especially arrangements that let you concentrate on one note at a time. Whichever option you've decided on, prepare to make sound the one point you focus on, the one point you come back to. Begin by putting on your tape or CD and trying Exercise X.

Exercise X
RELAXING TO SOUND

- Sit quietly and comfortably and take three deep breaths.
- For a few minutes let your mind run wild with whatever thoughts come up.
- Now close your eyes and begin to focus on the sounds in the room.
- Anytime you notice that you have drifted into thinking, bring your concentration back to the sound. Shifting your focus back to the sound will be both pleasant and calming.
- Spend as much time as you like listening to the tape or CD. When you're finished, take a few deep breaths and open your eyes.

While experimenting with sound as your point of focus, explore a variety of acoustics before deciding on your favorite one. Dozens of environmental tapes are available; and relaxing music runs the gamut from classical to gospel.

Random live sounds, like those produced by wind chimes, may also be effective.

Focusing on sound can be so absorbing that we end up merging with it—in other words, we become the sound. As the philosopher J. Krishnamurti put it: "We hardly ever listen to the sound of a dog's bark, or to the cry of a child or the laughter of a man as he passes by. It is this separation that is so destructive, for in that lies all conflict and confusion. The beauty is felt only when you and the sound are not separate, but when you are a part of it."[2] This sense of oneness can inspire deep serenity.

ONE POINT OF SEEING

One year on vacation, my wife and I were driving down a road in southern New Hampshire when we came upon an "Antiques" sign that directed us by way of a large red arrow down a dirt road. The tree-lined lane led to an old barn that had been converted into a store. Inside the store, I found a wagon wheel, its painted hub looking much like the sun. I couldn't tell if the sun was rising or setting, whether it signified the beginning or end of the day—which, I presume, was the point. Painted on each spoke of the wheel was a word or a phrase: "Family," "Right Livelihood," "Homestead," "Service to Others," "Unity of Humankind." Stepping back, I realized that the wagon wheel portrayed the facets of a person's life.

To this day, I can close my eyes and see that wagon wheel, right down to the words on its spokes. I think of it as the wheel of my life. There am I, Fred, in the middle. My sun is both rising and setting. As I contemplate the spokes, I can almost see how I'm doing in each area of my life. What's more, every spoke shows me how important all the others are if I am to move forward. Balance is essential or the wheel won't turn.

Whenever I concentrate on the wheel of my life, it becomes my sole point of focus and carries me into a state of deep relaxation. Although the wheel itself is no longer in my environment, it is in my mind's eye, where it remains eternally available to me. When I visualize it, I immediately become calm and reflective.

Exercise XI can help you move from merely seeing a point of focus to truly visualizing it. This is a two-part exercise: Part 1 involves staring open-eyed at an object, and Part 2 entails closing your eyes and re-creating in your mind's eye an image of that object. The object can be anything you choose. Look around the room and pick something. The exercise refers to a candle, although your object can just as well be a picture of your family, a flower arrangement, an icon, or anything else you enjoy looking at. If you like the idea of a candle, anything from a dinner candle to a birthday candle will do. Just set it on a table and light it.

Exercise XI
FIRST SEEING, THEN VISUALIZING

Part 1

- Sit back and take three deep breaths. Begin to breathe gently, and as you do, watch the flicker of the candle flame. When you become distracted by a thought, "watch" it go by as if watching a bus, rather than jumping on it and going for a ride. As the thought passes, bring your attention back to the flame.

- For a few seconds, keep your concentration on the candle flame, your one point of focus.

Part 2

- Close your eyes and "see" the image of the flame—not behind your eyelids, but in your mind's eye, the place in your head where thoughts play out like movies.
- Hold your concentration on the image of the flame. Anytime you notice that your mind has drifted away from this image, invite it to come back. Do not be harsh with yourself or judge your ability. Your mind will drift—there's no way around this phenomenon, as you well know.

While practicing Exercise XI, you may have to work with Part 1 for a while before achieving success with Part 2. Yet even when you move fully into Part 2, don't be surprised if the image changes after you close your eyes. In your mind's eye a candle flame can become a full moon, a sunrise, or any number of other sights. Let whatever happens, happen ... then stay with it as long as you can.

Staring open-eyed at a candle flame is a centuries-old

concentration practice. A more recent one has practitioners looking into a mirror for minutes at a time. This approach is said to awaken insight into oneself. Whichever point of focus you most enjoy working with, exercise your concentration muscle often, though not necessarily for extended periods of time. This technique will get easier with practice and a set routine—that's a promise.

8

Living Breath

Breath is a handy point of focus because it is with us constantly. In fact, we can't possibly leave home without it. Besides, it's been around a long time; even before we had our first taste of milk, we experienced our breath. Because breathing has been such a loyal companion throughout our lives, we tend to think we know it well.

Think again! Since you've started most of the previous

exercises by taking three deep breaths, you do know how soothing that can be. But there may be aspects of breathing you have never thought about. The exercises that follow can be used to engage your mind in some of these subtler experiences. Never again will you be able to take breathing for granted!

Exercise XII
THE TOUCH OF BREATH

While doing this exercise, keep your eyes open, keep reading, and keep breathing.

- Breathing easily, notice where the air enters and leaves your nostrils. In each instance you will be able to feel the spot where it first touches the inside of your nose. (If you can't breathe through your nose, separate your lips ever so slightly and feel where your breath touches them.)
- Continue to concentrate on your nostrils. Don't follow the air down into your throat or lungs; pay no attention

to how cold or warm the air is; disregard any odors you may notice. Just concentrate on the sensual, tactile feeling of friction that arises as the air brushes across the skin inside your nostrils while entering and leaving your nose.

- If you suddenly become conscious of the movement of your chest, bring your attention back to where the air is entering and leaving your nostrils. Feel it as it passes in and out…in and out.

- Become absorbed in the air entering and leaving your nostrils. Observe—but don't judge—whether your breaths are short or long. Continue breathing in and out…in and out.

- If your mind wanders, don't feel guilty. Just allow it to come back to where the air is entering and leaving your nostrils.

- Notice that each breath is divided into four parts: the inhale, a pause when your lungs are filled with air, the exhale, a pause when your lungs are empty of air. Continue breathing in and out…in and out.

- Do you sometimes "miss" the inhale, the exhale, or one

of the pauses because your mind has wandered away? If so, recognize that you were distracted and allow your mind to come back to the spot where you can feel the air entering and leaving your nostrils.

- After a while, observe your mind. Have your thoughts slowed down? Has a feeling of serenity begun to permeate your inner being?

This breath exercise will give you a point of focus as well as a sense of deep relaxation wherever you happen to be. Try it at work, for example, or while visiting a friend in the hospital, or while waiting to board a flight that's been delayed for two hours. Anytime you can't escape to the bathroom for a few minutes of peace and quiet, much less go for a walk in the woods, stop what you are doing and concentrate only on your nostrils. There's no need for explanations, since no one around you will know what you are doing!

The next two exercises can be done with your eyes either open or closed. If you are in public, consider keeping your eyes open. If you are at home, close them; that will deepen the experience for you.

Exercise XIII
WARMING THE AIR YOU BREATHE

- Sit quietly and take three deep breaths.
- Now breathe normally, feeling the breath in your nostrils as you did in Exercise XII.
- Notice the temperature of your breath as it enters and leaves through your nose. The air will soon feel cool upon entering your nostrils and warmer as it leaves your lungs.
- Continue to concentrate on the temperature of your breath.
- After a few minutes, observe that you are still concentrating on the temperature of your breath, and not on thinking.

Here's another possibility: breathe through your nose and listen to the sound your breath makes. If at first you can't hear it, take stronger and deeper breaths, then listen for the sound inside your head. On the inhale, the breath inside your head will sound like *haaa*; on the exhale, it will sound like *saaa*.

With a full breath, you will hear *haaa-saaa*. Think of it as the "silent whisper" of your breath.

Isn't it curious that your breath has been repeating the word-sounds haaa-saaa to you 35,000 times a day since the moment you were born and you never knew it? Well, the good news is that now you do know it and can tune in to this silent whisper anytime you want to. Better yet, it happens all by itself, with no effort on your part, as you will see in Exercise XIV.

Exercise XIV
THE SOOTHING VOICE IN YOUR HEAD

This point-of-focus exercise can quickly lead you into a state of deep relaxation.

- Sit comfortably and take three deep breaths.
- Breathing normally, pay attention to the *haaa* sound your breath makes as you inhale.
- While exhaling, hear the *saaa* sound.
- Continue to concentrate on the *haaa-saaa* of your

breath, listening quietly and calmly to this soothing voice in your head.

- After a few minutes, notice how much more relaxing this voice is than any other voice you may hear in your head.

All three of these breath exercises will help you reach a new level of calm. As you practice your favorite one, peacefulness will sink into you more deeply than before, and it will last longer. Luxuriate in this peacefulness. Hang out with it—take it to the Laundromat, the library, or out for pizza. Treat it well, because within it lie the seeds of self-confidence and a more positive attitude toward life.

9

Welcoming Words

One day my mother gave me a wallet card embossed with the Serenity Prayer.[3] She told me that when I got aggravated I should repeat this prayer; it would calm me down. By then I had learned to keep peace with my mother. Taking the card, I put it in my wallet, and the next day I threw it away. One of the things that aggravates me the most is being told what to do.

The Serenity Prayer

God, grant me the serenity to
accept the things I cannot change,
the courage to change the things I can,
and the wisdom to know the difference.

For many of us, childhood had religious overtones. Some of us were given a string of beads and a prayer to say over and over again for each one, as in the Catholic or Hindu faiths. Others of us thumbed through books of scriptures repeating page after page of prayers, as in the Jewish or Buddhist traditions. Whatever your childhood exposures were like, saying prayers over and over at this stage in your life could well become a form of relaxation. If you enjoyed it and did it because you wanted to, it may even lead to a mystical experience.

But if you, like me, did not enjoy saying prayers repeatedly, it could feel like a penance. If it does, jump to the bottom of page 68, or skip the rest of this chapter and go on to the next one.

The practice of repeating a set of words to calm down the

emotions has been around for as long as there have been words to repeat. Its calming effect comes from using words as a point of focus.

What set of words, if any, do you like to say over and over? What words bring you joy and guidance? A prayer from your youth, or perhaps a new one, such as the Prayer of St. Francis of Assisi or the Hebrew Shema?

Prayer of St. Francis of Assisi

Lord, make me an instrument of Thy peace;
where there is hatred, let me sow love;
where there is injury, pardon;
where there is doubt, faith;
where there is despair, hope;
where there is darkness, light;
and where there is sadness, joy.

O Divine Master,

grant that I may not so much
seek to be consoled, as to console;
to be understood, as to understand;
to be loved, as to love;

for it is in giving that we receive,
it is in pardoning that we are pardoned,
and it is in dying that we are born to eternal life.

Shema

She-ma Yis-ra-el	(Hear, O Israel)
A-do-noi El-o-ha-nu	(the Lord our God)
A-do-noi Eeh-had	(the Lord is One)

Whatever prayer you decide on, write it down and read it until you have it memorized. Then recite it each time you feel the steam of anxiety rising inside you.

✳

You can also recite a favorite poem, such as Robert Frost's "Stopping by Woods on a Snowy Evening," which ends with a repetition of the line "And miles to go before I sleep." If you like to sing, begin chanting your most-loved spiritual song, such as "Amazing Grace," which begins with the inspiring words "Amazing grace, how sweet the sound that saved a soul like me." When deciding on a poem or song to use as a point of focus, be sure to choose one that touches you. Then see what it does for your mind.

Remember, the techniques that suit the teacher may not suit the student, so don't be turned away by these particular examples. They are my favorite poems and songs. Use those that stir your soul.

10

Practice until You Want to Practice

Now that you are familiar with the whats and whys of relaxation practice, let's turn to the how-longs, wheres, and hows. You'll find the routine is much less tedious than you may expect. In fact, you're likely to discover that you can regularly practice your favorite exercise—or several of them— and still have a life!

How long should you practice?
Only five minutes in the morning and five minutes at night! No music teacher would say that two five-minute segments

a day could get you to Carnegie Hall. Nor would a baseball coach tell you this practice schedule could get you into the major leagues. Yet the fact remains that it will calm you down and it will change your life.

When I started reading books on relaxation, I was horrified to discover that I had to practice an hour a day or I would get nothing out of it. So I put the books down without even trying to build practice sessions into my life. Only later did I find out how wrong they were—at least for the beginner I was then.

Eventually, when I did start practicing, I aimed for five minutes morning and night, but I didn't always make it. Then slowly it started to become a habit, and now I practice most mornings and most evenings. Occasionally, I'll lose track of time and my practice will go longer than usual or be very brief. What matters is not so much the amount of time I devote to it as the pattern of consistently doing it.

Regularity is what breeds rewards—a formula I discovered while playing tennis. I'm not very good at the game, but because I like it I don't let my lack of proficiency stop me from heading for the courts. Every time I play, I reap great gains—sunshine, fresh air, and physical exercise. No way must

I be in the center court at Wimbledon to receive these fringe benefits; I need only make it a habit to lob the ball over the net a few times in a row. So it is with relaxation: after holding my point of focus for a few seconds and then starting over, I begin to feel good.

As you get into the five-minute morning and evening relaxation routine, you might like the changes you feel and eventually decide to extend your practice sessions. If so, all the better. For now, however, plan on five minutes at a stretch—preferably first thing in the morning, before your mind is filled with thoughts, and just before you go to bed at night. Calming yourself at the start of the day will help smooth the edges of the chaos to come; at the close of the day it will prepare you for a peaceful sleep.

Where should you practice?

Wherever you're most comfortable! The living room or the den will do just fine; or you might prefer to be outdoors under a tree, weather permitting. It often helps to have a spot set aside exclusively for your practice sessions. Although an entire room is ideal, the corner of a room will also work, as would any small space that is used for nothing else.

After a while you may want to begin decorating your spot. A special chair or cushion to sit on, or maybe a mat or pad, would make a good addition. Know that if you use the same couch, recliner, or rocking chair for relaxation that you sit in to watch Monday Night Football or to do needlepoint, you will still reap benefits from the practice. The key is comfort.

Nearby, you may want a small table to hold a candle, a picture, or flowers to look at, or the object you plan to hold. If you have not yet decided on an object to use as your point of focus, consider working with a rock or stick retrieved on a hike, or a seashell from a trip to the beach. Let the object help you re-create the place where you found it, which can then become the image for your visualization.

How should you practice?

First, take three deep breaths. As you begin to feel tranquil, move on to one of the longer exercises, such as counting backward; or imagining yourself at the seashore; or focusing on a touch, scent, taste, sound, sight; or repeating your favorite poem. Another possibility would be to concentrate on your inhale and exhale, listening to the *haaa-saaa* sound of your breath.

Try not to let noises distract you too much. If you're doing breath exercises in your living room and hear a motorcycle pass by, you may think, "I wonder what kind of bike that is. Who's driving? Where is the person going? Oh, it's the guy next door. He's going to the diner for breakfast... They have great pancakes at the diner...I'd really like some pancakes right now..." Next thing you know, your mind will have you enjoying breakfast while your body is still in the living room.

Rather than let the sound of the motorcycle instigate an entire adventure, allow it to pass by your house (and your mind), and return to breathing. In other words, as soon as you realize you have been distracted, come back to what you were doing.

Internal distractions are also possible, especially nagging questions. If you begin to wonder, for example, "Should I have lunch with Bill tomorrow?" answer with a yes or no, then get back to your practice. Do not allow your mind to negotiate the question or to weigh both sides pro and con. Your mind will try, but don't go there. Resisting the mind chatter by refocusing is a big part of the exercise. After you have practiced this technique for a while, once the question is answered it will leave you alone.

What if you want to practice in the afternoon,
and at other times too?

By all means, do so. The idea is to start with the consistency of a small block of time in the morning and at night, and then see how you like it. When you get good results, you may want to add a session at noon, or at sunset, or on a purely spontaneous basis. In other words, practice until you want to practice…then keep on practicing.

I used to practice breath exercises while sitting at my desk in the middle of a New York City advertising agency. Two of the people I worked for made me crazy, and the breathing techniques returned me to sanity. You can do this too. Here's how: while sitting at your desk, take thirty seconds to concentrate on the breath in your nostrils. Nothing else, just your breath. It will give you a break from the rut you're in and also clear your mind.

One day just before a meeting with difficult clients, I said to my boss, "Excuse me, I have to go to the bathroom."

(Anyone is allowed two minutes in the bathroom, I figured.) I closed the stall door, sat on the toilet, and visualized myself at the seashore. There I saw the waves, felt the sun, heard the gulls, and smelled the ocean air. I came back feeling quite refreshed!

If you excuse yourself to go to the "seashore" and then return to your office, the environment will be just as crazy as it was when you left. You, however, will have changed. You will see the situation differently, because you'll be a little more serene and a lot less caught up in other people's emotions.

As you bring the practice of relaxation into your everyday life, consider the wondrous opportunities offered not only by the bathroom but also by your car. To begin with, you could mentally convert your ignition key into your key to success. Just before you start your car—every time you start your car—stop and take three deep breaths. After you have stopped your car and turned off the ignition, take three deep breaths. Some people stick a red dot or gold star on their car key as a reminder to breathe.

These short pauses will change your attitude about driving. Soon both the anticipation of a nerve-racking commute and the aftermath of a frustrating one will no longer jangle your nerves. You'll cruise along happy to take in the scenery, and you'll return home with a smile.

Also try using your car as an auxiliary relaxation spot. Practice any of the point-of-focus exercises behind the steering wheel before leaving the car for an interview or before driving home from work. As for on-the-road practice, take a tip from Julia Cameron, author of *The Artist's Way*, who advises artists to refill their wells of creativity by changing their driving habits. Go for the mystery, she says. Substitute a new route for your usual one and you'll suddenly refocus on new sights in the visible world. Then you'll discover that "sight leads to insight."

Opportunities for spontaneous relaxation practice are endless. For instance, you could write the word "breathe" on the backs of several of your business cards or on little slips of paper. Tuck one of these "breathe cards" in your wallet or purse, another in your coat pocket, and a few more in the pockets of your shirt and pants. Then anytime you reach into your wallet or a pocket and come across a card, do what it says: take three deep breaths.

Use these techniques to relieve stress wherever and whenever it comes up. Stress, like vapors inside a teakettle, must be released from time to time; so as pressure mounts, let it out through relaxation. Teakettles, on the other hand, have no such option. With the buildup of too much steam, they squawk their heads off.

Practicing any of these relaxation techniques for even two minutes will remove your lid before you mouth off. So go ahead and take a two-minute breather at your desk or in the bathroom or in your car; then go back to everyday life. Your boss, the auto mechanic, your teenager, or whomever you are contending with will be as unreasonable as before. You, however, will be more calm, centered, and sane.

These techniques will work at the bus stop and on the loading dock. They'll work at midnight when you discover your exit is closed due to construction, and on the 747 when the landing gear makes that awful noise on its descent. This is how you can de-stress during stressful times.

PART THREE

Going Deeper

11

What Else
Is Cooking?

A few years ago I stopped eating meat—not because
some guru told me to, or to save the hogs and steers of the
world, or even to help redistribute the planet's food supply.
These are all admirable motives, but the reason I stopped eating meat was simply because I felt physically better that way.
I hoped to enjoy a better quality of life. That's also why I
practice relaxation: to have a better day, every day.

Soon after I changed my diet, a friend told me he didn't
eat red meat, so I asked him if he was a vegetarian. "Heck,

no!" he replied. "I don't eat my steaks red—I always have them well-done." That was the day I realized how important it was to understand what people mean by the terms they use. My friend steered clear of red meat, and I did too...but we were on different paths. In the end, however, both our paths led straight to the kitchen.

So it is with relaxation. If two people tell you they use biofeedback, for example, ask what they actually do and why. One person may say he's using it to help himself alter his brain-wave patterns or heart rate for purposes of stress management. The other may call it her tranquillity process. The stress management you will understand from having practiced the relaxation techniques in part 1 of this book. If you've trekked farther down the road into the point-of-focus exercises in part 2, you'll know about occupying the mind in order to achieve tranquillity. "Yes, I know about that," you might reply to each of these people. "I call it relaxation." Before you know it, you'll all be in the "calm-down kitchen" together discussing your favorite recipes for relaxation.

The point is that you're going to find differing terms and opinions about the pathways to relaxation. But there's no need to get proprietary about such matters. Just as you are likely to hear "My God is the only god" in discussions about religion, so are you apt to hear in conversations about relaxation, "If you're not doing it my way, you're not really doing it." Your job is to stay open-minded and understanding. Who knows—maybe you'll learn some helpful new techniques.

The cause for this counsel is that something else is cooking: we are about to embark on an adventure even farther down the road of relaxation. There are many names for this deeper practice. Dean Ornish, M.D., in his best-selling book *Eat More, Weigh Less,* calls it "meditation," and offers seven reasons for giving it a try:

> ➤ First, meditation can enhance your powers of concentration.
> ➤ Second, it can increase your awareness of what's going on around you.
> ➤ Third, it can increase your awareness of what's going on inside you.
> ➤ Fourth, it can quiet your mind, allowing you to experience "inner sources of peace, joy, and nourishment."
> ➤ Fifth, it can give you a clearer picture of yourself.

> Sixth, it can draw you into the present moment, helping you experience new ways of being.
> Last, and perhaps most important, "meditation can give you the direct experience of transcendence, perhaps the most powerful way to deal with isolation."[4]

Are these areas of life you would like to improve upon? If so—even if meditation is the last thing you're interested in exploring—take a deep breath and read on...The pot is boiling over with possibilities!

12

The "M" Word

We have been talking about calming down and relaxing, and Dean Ornish uses the "M" word—meditation. Is there a difference? Absolutely, and that's what you're about to discover. But first, let's pick up where we left off at the end of part 2.

Once you've gotten all tranquil and serene from your point-of-focus exercises, should you keep practicing? Yes, because if you stop, you'll begin to lose the benefits, and in a very short time you'll start feeling steam building up again in the teakettle. Keep practicing, however, and your mind will become a little quieter, a little less in need of being occupied.

After you've practiced for a while longer, you'll be able to sit quietly without concentrating on a point of focus. With no expectation of what might happen and no criticism of what does happen, you will cross the threshold into meditation and invite wondrous things to happen. But don't take my word for all this. Check it out yourself—practical experience is the best teacher. As world-renowned mythologist Joseph Campbell said when asked if he believed in a higher power, "I don't need to believe—I have experience."

You will see that when you go past point-of-focus exercises you'll reach a place of not doing anything. Not doing anything means not engaging your mind in a task of any sort. Although not thinking takes a lot of practice, you can do it; and you can go even further.

Ornish describes going further as "soul food." He tells us that although meditation is now used as a stress reducer, the ancient masters developed it for a different purpose—namely, to give people a direct experience of transcendence. "In this context," he explains, "meditation is food for your soul. It satiates the hunger that is not satisfied by food alone. When you directly experience the fullness of life, then you have less need to attempt to fill the void with food,"[5] or with anything else, for that matter.

Meditation is what happens in the gaps between thoughts. It also arises in the gaps between breaths, those pauses between the inhale and the exhale in which nothing happens—no inhaling, no exhaling, no thinking—if only for a second.

Now we are going to lengthen those gaps, extending the time span in which we are comfortable with nothing happening to occupy our minds. And strange as it may sound, we will accomplish this by doing nothing. "Why would I want to do that?" you may ask. Because this pause is the threshold to your true essence. And as you cross it, at least two other things will begin to happen. The first is that sooner or later you will feel a sense of connectedness to the world. The second result is that you will discover something very meaningful about your own place in the world. Together, these two experiences add up to self-revelation, or self-realization.

Here's a good way to think of it. If you go back to the example of the walk in the woods or the time spent in the garden, you'll recall that part of paying attention was the feeling you had of being connected to nature. With meditation, that feeling can expand to encompass the entire planet. As Native Americans say, the earth—our "Mother Earth"—is a living, breathing organism whose breath expands (as in hurricanes, floods, and typhoons) and contracts (as in earthquakes). Because we humans are also living, breathing organisms, and because we are sustained by the earth, we are able to feel our connection to it.

For me, holding on to this feeling of connectedness is much easier in the woods than at home in the middle of the city. Yet no matter where I am, the feeling is accessible to me through meditation. I simply go to my center and do nothing, as in Exercise XV. This is an exercise without a point of focus. Since it is inner directed, you won't be expecting tangible results. It helps if you also don't critique what comes up; just observe it and see what comes up next.

Exercise XV
GOING DEEPER

This journey into meditation will help you feel a deep sense of connectedness to the world. First, read it through to learn what it's about. Then try it while reading the instructions. The third time, close your eyes and do the exercise while talking yourself through it.

- Sit back and relax. Take three deep breaths.
- Place your left hand over your lower abdomen and your right hand over your left hand. Feel the gentle rise and fall of your lower abdomen as you inhale and exhale.
- Take a few more breaths, then close your eyes.
- Become aware of the spot where your breath enters and leaves your nostrils. Continue to concentrate on this spot as you take a few more breaths.
- Now begin to follow your breath with your attention. Inhale, and as you do, feel the air in your nose, all the while seeing it in your mind's eye. Feel the breath as it goes up from your nostrils to the top of your head, and

then down a vertical passageway to a spot behind your hands. Feel the gentle rise of your lower abdomen under your hands.

- Exhale, and as you do, feel the breath move up the passageway to the top of your head and out through your nostrils. Feel the lowering of your abdomen under your hands.
- Inhale…in and down to your central core behind your hands. Exhale…up from your central core and out your nostrils.
- Take a few more breaths.
- While continuing to breathe slowly, feel and "see" the place behind your hands.
- Take a few more breaths.
- Now stop focusing on your breath and simply feel and "see" the gentle rise and fall of your lower abdomen.
- Take a few more breaths.
- Next, stop focusing on the rise and fall of your lower abdomen and instead feel and "see" your center, the spot behind your hands.
- Take a few more breaths.
- Finally, drop your attention down to your center.

Rather than being in your head looking down at your abdomen, step into an imaginary internal elevator and press the "down" button; ride down until you are behind your palms. In other words, don't look down there—be there. Breathe and be there, waiting to see what happens.

- Take many breaths, all the while trying to feel for an inner vibration at the core of your being. This vibration is very subtle.

13

The Stuff of
the Universe

The first promise of meditation, as we learned in chapter 12, is that it brings a feeling of connectedness with the world. It dispels the sense of aloneness.

Have you ever been through a time of feeling all alone? Do the following sentiments sound familiar to you?

My separateness, my aloneness, has always been with me and is here now, a recurring theme that has continuously run through my life. My closeness with Mama didn't

change it. ... Aloneness is an inner state... Even now, with
my three beautiful daughters, my two sweet sons, and my
wonderful, sexy husband, deep down inside I am still profoundly alone.[6]

That is the voice of Diana Ross, as chronicled in her
memoir, *Secrets of a Sparrow*. If Diana Ross—one of the
wealthiest, most talented, and most beautiful women in
America—feels profoundly alone, what chance do you and I
have of feeling otherwise?

To be sure, there are times when I feel all alone. Oh, I'm
married to a woman I love deeply, my parents are still living,
and I have friends; but I sometimes feel a gnawing emptiness
inside me, a sense of "not belonging" in the world. On a
deep-down level, my wife can't make me feel okay. Neither
can my parents or friends. Nor can my job or my bank
account or a new car, or the jacket I bought last week. The
jacket was great the day I bought it, and even the first few
times I wore it, but soon afterward, being the proud owner of
this beautiful jacket did not help me feel like a valued mem-
ber of society. The new car made me feel good for several
weeks, but sure enough, that thrill wore off too.

So, what shall I do? Buy a new jacket each week and a car every month? Trade in my wife every five or ten years? (What if she decides to trade me in for a younger, richer, better-looking model of a husband?) Even if I get a promotion at work, the feeling of fulfillment will last only a little while. Then I'll need another promotion, and another, until I'm the CEO. At that point I'll need to find a bigger company so I can become CEO of that one.

The search for "more," "bigger," "better," and "different" will soon have me chasing my own tail. How many jobs, cars, and wives must I go through before realizing that my life is not working, that I've done everything the television commercials told me to do and I'm no more fulfilled than I was at the start?

How can I make my life work? Simple—by meditating and connecting to an inner source. After all, if I can't get what I need from the outside, the only place left is inside.

With meditation, remember, we're beyond thinking. We're feeling the other stuff—the essence that dwells within us. This "feeling" is actually a knowing that oozes through every cell of our being. It may not be an overwhelming feeling, and it may come on just a little at a time, yet however it happens we don't think our way into it. Through meditation, we know it.

That's what happened for me after slipping between my thoughts and dropping down to the center of my being. A few weeks into this practice I found a vibration of unity—primal unity. Not the primal aloneness I experience when I'm up in my head, but a unity with all things... and I do mean all things.

This vibration is hard to describe, so I'll portray it conceptually. Quantum physicists tell us that the space between the atoms of our bodies is composed of the same "stuff" that makes up the space between the planets in our solar system and the space between the solar systems in our galaxy. It's the same stuff that makes up the space in the entire universe! The vibration that came to me in meditation assured me that I am composed of the same stuff as the universe. Just as I had felt connected to nature while in the woods, I could now feel connected to all that is—a oneness with all things in the universe.

Define the meaning of stuff however you will. A religious person would say that it is God, that they have a piece of God inside them, that their soul is a piece of God, that they are a child of God, and that they are connected to all living beings in the universe because of their connection to God. A mystical or spiritual person might say there is an all-pervading spirit that is in and of the universe, and is therefore a part of us. Wallace D. Wattles, an early-twentieth-century self-help author in the "new thought movement," once wrote, "There is a thinking stuff from which all things are made, and which, in its original state, permeates, penetrates, and fills the interspaces of the universe."[7]

All the energy in the universe is the same. Name it whatever you like; call it "God" or "stuff" or anything you wish. The point is that you don't need a religion to discover the existence of this energy. All it takes is meditation—dropping down inside and being there with no expectation of what might arise and no criticism of what does arise. Just feel the vibration and take it as it comes.

14

Your Place
in It All

The last chapter may have seemed a little thick or dense to you. That's because it is. But don't let that deter you forever. If these notions of energy and vibration are too mumbo-jumbo for you, forget this section for now and come back to it in six months or a year. The words may have a different ring to them after you've practiced relaxation techniques for a while longer. Till then, remember these words from T. K. V. Desikachar: "The ultimate goal of meditation is to always observe things accurately. It brings more clarity and compassion into our lives."[8] And, once in a while, remind yourself how far you have come in a short time.

Here's a brief recap: remember that in addition to feeling a connectedness to the world, the other phenomenon that sooner or later will arise in meditation is an answer to the age-old question, "What is my place in the world?"

At some point, every person wonders, "What am I supposed to be doing with my life?" Native Americans go on vision quests to find answers to this dilemma, monks spend days in prayer, and some people pay through the nose for years of therapy. But meditation too can give us an intuitive idea of what's best for us. We need only *listen* for an answer to this question. We would do well to phrase it in more immediate terms, such as, "What should I do today?"

Intuition is like a muscle—the more we exercise it, the stronger and more reliable it becomes. Moreover, occasional hunches quickly turn into knowledge deep inside us. When you are ready, go back to Exercise XV and see what bubbles up.

In addition, meditation can help you remember what you are not. For example, you are not your mind. You are also not your job; you do your job, but you are not your job. Neither are you anything else outside of you, such as your house or spouse, or your parent or child. Although you may love these aspects of your life, and even wear them like a badge of honor, they are not you. Meditation allows you to step back and observe these aspects of your life as if you were watching a program on television and not actually being in the program, living it. Meditation gives us a new perspective on our lives.

Here's another benefit of meditation: by staying with the feeling that you are part of the universe, you will come to a feeling of "having enough." No longer will you think you need, like I did, more jobs, cars, jackets, and wives. Instead, you will have switched from a mind-set of competition for the little there is in the world to one of gratitude for all that is, knowing that in fact there is more than enough. All of this is waiting for you on the inside…whenever you are ready, give deeper meditation a try.

15

Tune in to Your Life

Have you ever missed dinner? I don't mean because you were too busy to eat or too late getting home; I mean while you were sitting right there at the dinner table with your family or friends.

I have. I am capable of tasting only the first bite of dinner, because after that my mind is off and running. "You eat dinner," it says. "I've got some thinking to do." (Remember breathing and counting at the same time?) Then before I know it, my plate is empty, dinner is over... and having paid no attention to it, I missed the entire feast!

To prevent such distractedness, cultures around the world begin their meals with a prayer of thankfulness for the food set before them. Dean Ornish would call this "eating as meditation." In his words, "There is an old Zen saying, 'How you do anything is how you do everything.' When you rush through meals, you are likely to rush through life. ... When you can practice eating with awareness, then you are more likely to begin living with greater awareness. In this context, meditation not only enhances the experience of eating; eating with awareness becomes a form of meditation." [9]

How many other day-to-day experiences do you miss because you're not paying attention? When approached with awareness, those too become forms of meditation. In fact, life itself is a meditation. Actually, life is *the* meditation—the big one. It's happening now, with or without us. As John Lennon once sang, "Life is what happens to you while you're busy making other plans."

Meditation—paying attention one moment at a time—happens in the gap between thoughts. That's where we notice what's going on. Otherwise we're thinking, and not paying attention. When I am thinking, I'm not in the present moment; I'm not living my life; I'm living in the past or in the future. When I am paying attention, what happened yesterday does not matter; what matters is the present moment, each present moment.

By not paying attention, we can lose great chunks of our lives. Our parents tell us to take pictures of our kids, for example. We nod and say yes, and the next thing we know, it's their high school graduation and we haven't taken pictures for the last seventeen and a half years. If that's true of you, stop and smell your children.

The challenge is to live your life one moment at a time. Whether you believe you have only one life to live or a series of them, live this one as if it were your one and only life.

Lack of attention can be remedied by what Buddhists call mindfulness. When you are in the state of mindfulness, you find meaning—worthwhileness—in everything you do, because you do it completely, wholeheartedly. To achieve this mindful way of being, simply tune in to whatever it is you are doing. When you are walking in the woods, just walk, rather than trying to get somewhere. Move along with the mind of a child, experiencing wonderment upon seeing a flower, a colored leaf, a small animal scurrying by.

The best way to move into this state of heightened awareness is to practice paying attention one moment at a time. Eventually, your relaxation practice will lead naturally into meditation practice. So begin paying attention in the morning while you're in your meditation spot, far from worldly distractions. Think of this morning practice as a rehearsal for the rest of the day.

In time, you'll be able to practice meditating while out in the world. For instance, when your spouse, boss, or a friend speaks to you, avoid the temptation to prepare your reply and then jump in with it when the other person stops to take a breath. Instead, listen to that person completely, word for word, and then formulate your response. Think of this approach as paying attention one word at a time.

Lest you imagine that your new silence might be seen as lack of interest, remember the words of J. Krishnamurti, who considered this form of mindfulness a path to true understanding. He wrote, "Meditation is not an escape from the world; it is not an isolating, self-enclosing activity, but rather the comprehension of the world and its ways."[10]

Taoists, followers of sixth-century B.C. Chinese philosophy, also speak of this phenomenon. They say there is an invisible, unspoken Way in which the world unfolds, and our job is to come into harmony with it. But if it's invisible and nobody talks about it, you may ask, how can we come into harmony with it? Here, again, the answer is: by paying attention. When we tune in to the world around us, we discover there is a pulse in things inanimate as well as animate. For example, while operating a machine, such as a car or sewing machine, we may at first think we're the ones in control, but actually we're working in partnership with the machine. Although we may read the owner's manual, the machine itself is apt to be the best teacher. Each unit—even though it comes off an assembly line and seems identical to thousands of others—possesses a unique energy and set of characteristics. When we pay close attention to the machine, it will tell us how it performs best and how it "wants" to be used. Sure, we can try to impose our will on it, but the results are likely to be disappointing. If we relax and feel our way while driving the car, for instance, we will soon come into harmony with it. If we try to make it work the way we want it to—if we try to push the river, so to speak—the outcome may be disastrous. The same is true of a sewing machine. The larger the machine, the more obvious this becomes. Imagine driving not a family passenger car, but an eighteen-wheeler. I would truly want to be in harmony with something that heavy, lest I lose "control." Next, how about seeing yourself as the operator of an extremely large Caterpillar tractor or a four-story-tall construction crane? Would it be wise for me to force these machines to do my will, my way, or better for me to learn to work as a co-active partner with them to get the job done safely?

Another example of a seemingly inanimate object is a house. I'm not talking about the Stephen King kind of houses, the ones that are haunted and swallow up uninvited explorers. I mean my house, your house, or the one next door to you. I noticed this pulse when my wife and I moved into our first home, which we remodeled. If you've ever remodeled a house, you know that some parts of the job go smoothly, whereas others, sometimes the simplest repairs, for whatever reasons, take much longer than estimated. In our case, it was as if the house had a life as well as a will of its own. Only by not trying to force something to happen faster or sooner, but instead trying to help the structure evolve in its own way, could we free ourselves of the daily headaches of constantly thinking we were falling behind schedule. Instead we came to realize we were helping to create the best possible house it could become. As in other areas of my life, if I tried to make a situation go my way it either didn't at all or took much longer than my game plan called for. And that appears to be the lesson of all of life itself. If we remain sensitive to our surroundings, we soon fall into the natural rhythm of living. When I'm not paying attention to what's going on around me, for example, I "bump into" life, in the form of a doorjamb or the rear end of the car in front of me. If I'm paying attention to my surroundings instead of trying to push the river, I have an easier time of it.

Thought and action go hand in hand to make us who we are. Why is this so? Because who we are today is a result of what we did in the past. Similarly, who we will become is a result of our current thoughts, since what we think ultimately determines what we will do. Hence, we think…we act…we become.

It follows that the great changes we would like to make in our lives result from the changes we bring to our thinking. And if our thinking is negative, the easiest way to effect desirable results is through positive actions.

This may sound roundabout, but watch how it works. If you have negative thoughts about yourself and would like to deepen your self-respect, behave (positive actions) in ways that will increase your respect for yourself (positive thinking).

One positive action that can profoundly influence who you will become is the practice of relaxation techniques that will sooner or later lead you into meditation. All the benefits of calming down will flow through you, including a quiet mind, serenity, and inner peace. In this frame of mind you will feel good inside and deeply connected to the world around you, leading eventually to positive actions and a new you.

POINTS TO REMEMBER

Don't confuse techniques with meditation. Counting backward and watching a candle flame are relaxation techniques; meditation happens in the pause between breaths. Meditation happens as you go past techniques and out of thought.

Meditation happens as you mindfully live your life, paying attention to each moment.

Life is the meditation. Good days, bad days, it's your life—live every moment of it!

Even if you're absolutely, totally nuts today, tomorrow you can revel in peace of mind.

Well, there you have it. A game plan, a blueprint, a call to action for a more peaceful and enjoyable life. As I promised at the beginning of our journey, my hope is that these baby steps we took together, simple and easy exercises, will help you move into a more comfortable way of living. You may want to reread the seemingly denser sections of this book. They will come to serve you well, just as three deep breaths will serve you well for the rest of your life. Thank you for making me a part of your life. It has truly been my pleasure to travel a short distance on the road with you.

Namaste...I honor the spirit in you!

Notes

1. T. K. V. Desikachar, *The Heart of Yoga* (Rochester, VT: Inner Traditions International, 1995), p. 115.

2. J. Krishnamurti, *Meditations* (Boston: Shambhala, 1991), p. 22.

3. Copyright © 1962 Reinhold Niebuhr—American theologian, 1892–1971.

4. Dean Ornish, *Eat More, Weigh Less* (New York: HarperCollins, 1993), pp. 74–75.

5. *Ibid.,* p. 78.

6. Diana Ross, *Secrets of a Sparrow: Memoirs* (New York: Villard, 1993), p. 229.

7. Wallace D. Wattles, *The Science of Getting Rich* (Lakemont, GA: Copple House, 1975), p. 110.

8. T. K. V. Desikachar, *The Heart of Yoga,* p. 118.

9. Dean Ornish, *Eat More, Weigh Less,* p. 73.

10. J. Krishnamurti, *Meditations,* p. 31.

About the Author

FRED L. MILLER is an author, coach, and teacher. He spent twenty-five years in television production, a life that drove him absolutely nuts until he learned to calm down. He has written for prime-time network television and produced and directed documentary and educational films. His stint at a large New York advertising agency is what almost put him over the edge.

Fred speaks and conducts workshops and classes nationwide. Having spent twenty years acquiring esoteric knowledge, he has devoted the last ten to making that knowledge accessible in everyday terms. He lectures on breath awareness at the UCLA School of Medicine and is certified by the California State Bar Association to teach attorneys meditation as stress management. Also, Blue Cross of California lists him as a preferred provider in complementary medicine.

How to Calm Down: Three Deep Breaths to Peace of Mind
Have questions? Want to learn more?
Ask: fred@howtocalmdown.com.
www.howtocalmdown.com